Fire Management and Invasive Plants

A Handbook

by Matthew Brooks
U.S. Department of the Interior
U.S. Geological Survey
Western Ecological Research Center

and

Michael Lusk
National Wildlife Refuges
Invasive Species Coordinator
4401 N. Fairfax Dr., Rm. 655B
Arlington, VA 22203

Acknowledgements:

We would like to thank the following people for their contributions to the publication of this Handbook. Jenny Ericson for general project oversight. Karen Murphy, Fred Wetzel, Bill Leenhouts, and Karen Phillips for their numerous reviews of the document and resulting edits. Mara Weisenberger for proofreading and editing the document and supplying photos. Sue Wilder for gathering information on fire and invasive species policy. Karen Miranda Gleason and Kevin Kilbride for providing background information. Brian McManus, Chris Pease, Art Latterell and Andy Loranger for their continued support of the project and help in moving the project to completion. Aaron Fester for editing the document to make it more accessible to the field. Mark Newcastle for layout, format and design. The compilation and synthesis of information and the final production of this Handbook was supported by funding from the U.S. Fish and Wildlife Service, National Refuge System, Branch of Fire Management; U.S. Geological Survey, Invasives and Ecosystems programs; and numerous projects administered by the Joint Fire Science Program, most notably project #00-1-2-04.

Suggested citation:

Brooks, M. and M. Lusk. 2008. *Fire Management and Invasive Plants: a Handbook.* United States Fish and Wildlife Service, Arlington Virginia, 27 pp.

Table of Contents

Executive Summary and General Recommendations

Fire management can help maintain natural habitats, increase forage for wildlife, reduce fuel loads that might otherwise lead to catastrophic wildfire, and maintain natural succession. Today, there is an emerging challenge that fire managers need to be aware of: invasive plants. Fire management activities can create ideal opportunities for invasions by nonnative plants, potentially undermining the benefits of fire management actions.

This manual provides practical guidelines that fire managers should consider with respect to invasive plants.

What's the Link Between Fire and Plant Invasion?

The growth and spread of any plant species depends on two main factors:

1) plant propagule availability: the abundance of seeds and other plant propagules (i.e., parts of a plant that can produce a new individual), and

2) plant resource availability: the amount and quality of resources (sunlight, soil nutrients, etc.) that newly arrived propagules need to grow.

Postfire conditions can create ideal habitat for certain plants. When those conditions are created within easy range of the propagules of invasive plants, the situation is ripe for an invasion. The graphs below (Box 1.) illustrate both invasion potential and subsequent management strategy based on the relationship between plant propagule availability and resource availability.

What Can Fire Managers Do?

The best approaches fire managers can take for reducing the potential for invasive plant infestations are to minimize or eliminate the introduction of invasive plant propagules into fire management areas and minimize the amount of resources available to any such plants that might find their way into the burned area.

Primary Guidelines

At a minimum, the following should be applied in all situations:

- **Prevent Dispersal of Invasive Plants:**
  - Locating fire camps and staging areas in areas relatively free of weeds and other invasive plants.

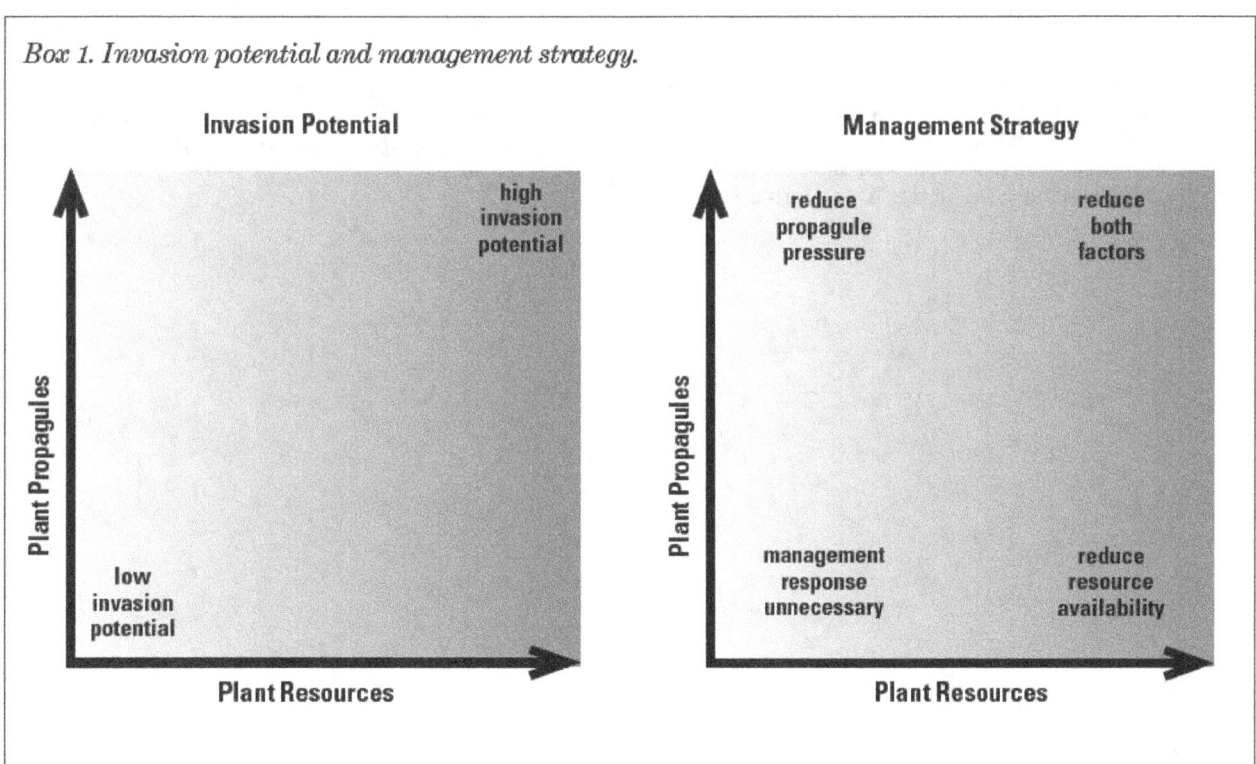

Box 1. Invasion potential and management strategy.

Invasion Potential

high invasion potential

Plant Propagules

low invasion potential

Plant Resources

Management Strategy

reduce propagule pressure

reduce both factors

Plant Propagules

management response unnecessary

reduce resource availability

Plant Resources

- Washing vehicles and equipment before and after being used within a project area (i.e., treatment area, fireline).
- Ensuring that any revegetation (i.e., seed mixes) or other organic material (i.e., straw mulch) that is introduced into the project area is certified as weed-free.

- **Minimize Resources Available to Invasive Plants:**
  - Remove only enough vegetation to accomplish the management objectives (i.e., creating a managed fuel zone, constructing a fireline).
  - As an alternative to vegetation removal, consider replacing highly flammable vegetation with less flammable vegetation when creating a managed fuel zone.

Are Additional Steps Necessary?

The above guidelines should be applied to all situations. You will need more information—primarily regarding propagule and resource availability—to determine if additional preventative methods are necessary. In these cases, fire managers need to prioritize which actions will provide the best results, and these actions can vary depending on the circumstances associated with each individual fire. Consult the reference guide below that includes additional site-based guidelines providing more specific recommendations associated with four typical scenarios.

1. Low Propagule Availability and Low Resource Availability

No major management actions are warranted.

- Low propagule availability can occur if survey data indicate few populations and low densities of invasive plants.
- Low resource availability can occur where vegetation loss is relatively low and/or recovery potential is high. Examples include fuels projects that thin but do not completely remove vegetation or fires where burn severities are relatively low

and/or native vegetation cover is expected to reestablish within a few years.

- Almost all management actions have the potential to cause unexpected and undesirable effects (i.e., seed mixes or straw mulch can be contaminated by unwanted species), so they should only be implemented if there are compelling reasons to do so.

2. Low Propagule Availability and High Resource Availability

Management actions should focus on minimizing resource availability.

- In this scenario resource availability is high, such as following complete removal of vegetation to create managed fuel zones or after a high severity fire. If the area has high levels of resource availability, then it may be most effective to focus management efforts on reducing these factors. However, the absence or rarity of invasive plants may warrant little or no additional management response.

3. High Propagule Availability and Low Resource Availability

Management actions should focus on minimizing propagule availability.

- If the area in question is in proximity to large source populations of invasive plants, then management of propagule dispersal into the area may be the best strategy. Focus on preventing the dispersal of propagules into the project areas, and on eradicating newly established individuals and populations at the edges of the invasive plants' range. Follow-up monitoring is always required to determine if re-treatment is needed.

4. High Propagule Availability and High Resource Availability

Management actions are warranted to minimize both plant propagule availability and resource availability as discussed above.

Using fire as a tool to manage at the landscape scale. Photo by M. Weisenberger, USFWS.

Box 2. Summary of Guidelines.

Low Propagule/Low Resource *No major management actions are warranted where* ▪ Vegetation loss from fire is low ▪ Native vegetation is expected to return quickly	**Low Propagule/High Resource** *Management actions should focus on minimizing resource availability where* ▪ Native vegetation is completely removed but invasive plants are rare or absent from the area.
High Propagule/Low Resource *Management actions should focus on minimizing propagule availability where* ▪ Area in question is in proximity to large source populations of invasive plants.	**High Propagule/High Resource** *Management actions are warranted to minimize both plant propagule availability and resource availability as discussed above where* ▪ Native vegetation is completely removed (fuel load management, severe wildfire), *and* invasive propagules have access to the area.

Section I
Introduction

The purpose of this manual is to provide practical guidelines for fire managers to effectively integrate invasive plant management activities into their fire management programs. Traditionally, fire management and invasive plant management have been conceived and implemented as separate programs. This manual is designed to help land managers bridge the gap between these two disciplines, and in particular give fire managers the tools they need to integrate invasive plant management strategies into the fire planning process. Although this handbook is tailored specifically for the fire management community within the National Wildlife Refuge System of the U.S. Fish and Wildlife Service, it is also relevant to other agencies and organizations that manage wildland fire.

U.S. Fish and Wildlife Service fire crew conducting a prescribed burn. USFWS.

Section II
Definitions

One of the potentially confusing aspects of invasive plant management relates to definitions. Many different terms have been associated with plants that are land management problems or deemed undesirable for one reason or another. Because these terms are often used interchangeably in management documents, and their usage can be confusing, some of the most commonly used terms are defined below. Several commonly used fire management terms are also described to encourage consistency across programs.

Accidentally Introduced. Species that dispersed without intentional human intervention, such as contaminants of plant stock or planting materials (i.e., mulches), or by attaching to equipment, shoes, or animals.

Deliberately Introduced. Species that were intentionally transported to and cultivated in new areas for various purposes such as livestock forage, erosion control, or ornamental horticulture, but then subsequently spread into areas where they are unwanted.

Fire Behavior. The rate of spread, residence time, flame length, and flame depth of an individual fire.

Fire Hazard. Fuel conditions that are deemed hazardous to human life, property, or valued land management resources (i.e., natural, cultural, recreational).

Fire Regime. Defined by type (ground, surface, or crown fire), frequency (i.e., return interval), intensity, severity, size, spatial complexity, and seasonality of fire within a given geographic area or vegetation type.

Fuel Zone. A defined area within which fuels are managed to influence fire behavior and/or fire regimes.

Invasibility or Invasion Potential. The tendency of a landscape (plant community, ecosystem, or geographic region) to being invaded.

Invasion. In this handbook, the term is used to mean both the: 1) spread and establishment of new species into an area they did not previously occupy; and 2) increase in dominance (i.e., % density, cover, and/or biomass) of species previously present but relatively uncommon within an area.

Invasiveness. The tendency of a species to successfully invade a landscape.

Fuel types and weather conditions contribute to fire behavior. Photo by M. Weisenberger, USFWS.

Invasive Species. Federal Agencies are encouraged to use the definition of invasive species established by Executive Order 13112. By this definition invasive species are both nonnative to the region of interest and cause environmental or economic harm or harm to human health.

Management Unit. This term is used in this handbook as a generic term that refers to a specific area of interest. These areas of interest typically include individual postfire management projects, fire management units (FMUs) or the entire area encompassed by a fire management plan.

Nonnative. This term refers to species that are not native to a particular ecosystem. It provides a more objective criterion than the term weed. Other terms that have been used as synonyms for nonnative

include alien, exotic, introduced, non-indigenous, acclimatized, adventive, escaped, feral, foreign, naturalized, immigrant, and xenobiotic.

Plant Propagules. Parts of plants (i.e., seeds, rhizomes, tubers, etc.) that are capable of independent propagation of a new individual.

Plant Resources. Physical resources that can limit plant growth, primarily including sunlight, water, and mineral nutrients.

Weed. To qualify as a weed, a plant only needs to be considered out of place or otherwise unwanted where it is currently growing. In wildland settings the term weed is not sufficient and a more specific definition is required.

A prescribed burn at Chesapeake Marshlands National Wildlife Refuge Complex. Photo by Gerald Vickers, USFWS.

Section III
How Do Plant Invasions Occur?

Plant invasions can occur for several reasons. The type of habitat disturbance, proximity to previously invaded sites, the number and means available to spread propagules, altered resource levels, and disruption of ecological processes have all been associated with invasive plants spreading into new areas. All of these factors can be broadly lumped into two primary variables (See Figure 1):

1. the availability of plant propagules; and

2. the availability of plant resources.

Plant Propagules

When considering plant propagule availability, it is important to consider the species they represent in addition to their abundance. If numerous propagules reach an area, but their specific characteristics are not adapted to the local environment, they are not likely to establish a population. Even if propagules are well suited for establishing and reproducing in a new environment, they still may not establish a population if the initial number of propagules is too small.

In contrast, if many propagules disperse that are compatible in a new environment, then a new population is likely to establish. Propagules can be introduced deliberately (i.e., added to postfire seeding mixes) or accidentally (i.e., contaminant species in postfire seeding mixes or straw mulch) (Fig. 2, link A). Plant propagule numbers can be reduced by seed predators (i.e., mice, squirrels, and many birds) or diseases that reduce the reproductive rates of invasive plants. Established invasive populations can spread locally, creating a feedback loop that can become problematic (Fig. 2, link C).

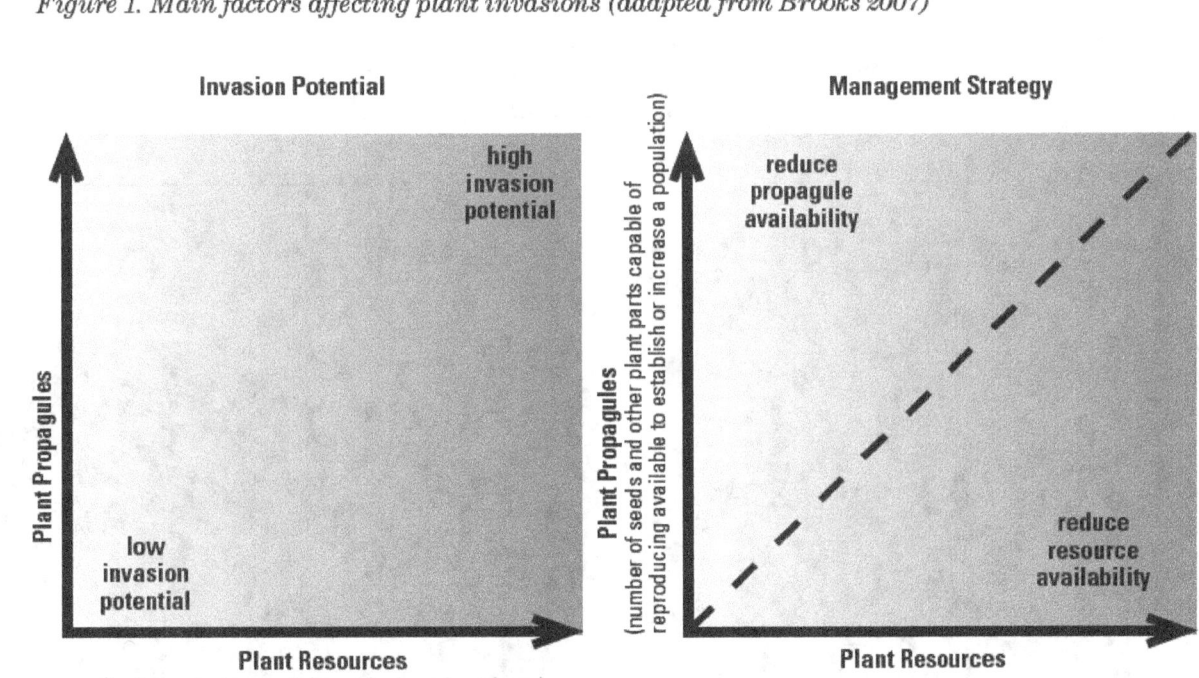

Figure 1. Main factors affecting plant invasions (adapted from Brooks 2007)

A Recipe for Trouble
Invasive potential is highest when propagules of invasive plants are likely to reach new areas that offer the combination of resources (soil nutrients, sunlight and moisture) necessary to establish and compete with native plants for these resources.

Resource Availability

In vegetation types where there is frequent natural disturbance, native vegetation is often able to recover quickly (i.e., by resprouting or establishing from seed), and therefore high resource availability following disturbance may not be a factor in invasive plant populations becoming established.
In other vegetation types, plant resource availability, particularly soil nutrients, can affect whether invasive plants become established. Following a fire, such resources can be increased directly, (i.e., postfire fertilization) or indirectly from the sudden reduced competition for nutrients after vegetation is removed (Fig. 2, link B).

Established populations of invasive plants can affect the supply of resources available (Fig. 2, link D). For example, some invasive plants might limit the growth of other species through competition or inhibition of nutrient uptake.

Processes that reduce plant resource availability, such as postfire recovery of vegetation, can reduce invasion potential. As vegetation recovers, resource uptake increases.

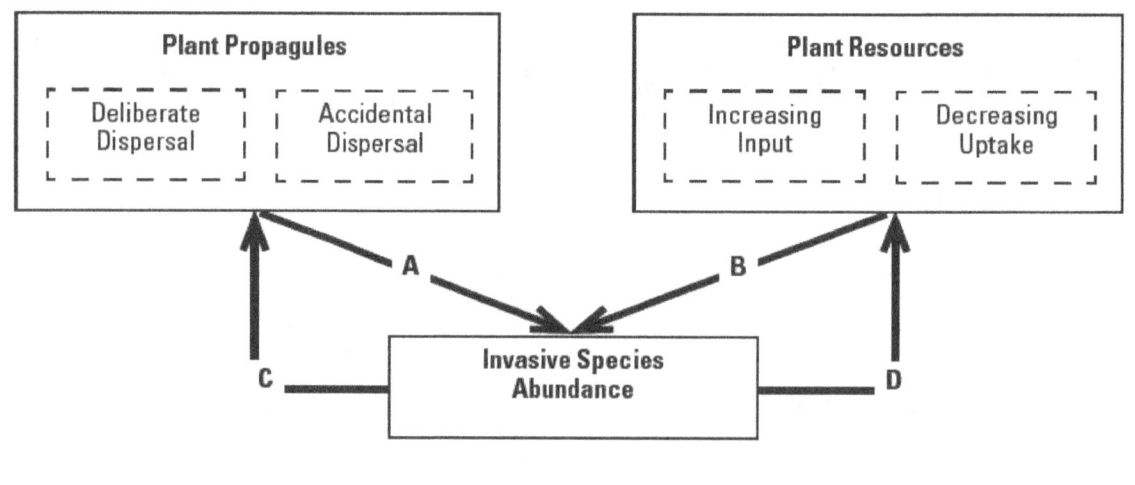

Figure 2. Relationships between propagule availability, resource availability, and invasive species abundance (adapted from Brooks 2007). Plant propagules (A) and plant resources (B) both affect the abundance of nonnative plant populations. Once these populations are established, they can affect plant propagules (C) and plant resources (D).

Regrowth of grass postfire. Photo by M. Weisenberger, USFWS

Golden crownbeard (Verbesina encelioides) regrowth following a prescribed burn in pinyon-juniper habitat. Photo by M. Weisenberger, USFWS.

Section IV

Why Should the Management of Invasive Plants and Fires Be Combined?

There are three general reasons why management of invasive plants should be combined with the management of fires:

1) Fires can promote plant invasions.

2) Fire can be used as a tool to control plant invasions.

3) Plant invasions can affect fuels, fire behavior, and fire regimes.

1. Fires Can Promote Plant Invasions

Fires can quickly and dramatically change the landscape and alter the competitive balance within the biotic community. Fires consume plant biomass, which increases the availability of light and reduces the consumption of soil nutrients, thus increasing invasion potential during at least the first few postfire years (Fig. 2).

Most invasions by nonnative plants that have been reported in the scientific literature report situations where invasive plants were already established within landscapes prior to fire. However, disturbance as a result of a fire event served as an opportunity for invasive plants to expand their local distributions and dominance.

Although fire may not be necessary for an invasive plant to become established in an area, it may allow the population to expand to the point that it harms the local ecosystem. From an ecological standpoint and from the perspective of land managers, such negative effects represent the area of greatest concern, and may require a response.

In some native vegetation types that are fire dependent (i.e., chaparral), increased dominance of invasive plants may be fleeting; native vegetation quickly recovers and outcompetes invasive plants. Where native vegetation is not dependent on fire, however, the plants do not respond fast enough, allowing invasive plants to establish and spread (i.e., some desert shrublands).

Thus, the effects of fire on the spread of invasive populations can depend on the biology of the native vegetation, such as the rate at which it recovers following fire.

Burning piles of Russian thistle (Salsola *spp.*) *to control seed dispersal. Photo by M. Weisenberger, USFWS.*

2. Fire Can be Used to Control Plant Invasions

Fire has been used since pre-historic times to manage vegetation for various purposes. Modern use of fire in wildland areas has focused on treatments to reduce hazardous fuel loads, restore historical disturbance regimes, improve forage and habitat for game and livestock, promote biodiversity, and manage nonnative invasive plants. Much of what is currently known about using fire to control invasive plants has been derived from studies of cropland systems. Unfortunately, there are many fundamental differences between cropland and wildland settings, and our ability to use information derived from croplands to predict effects that may occur in wildlands is limited.

Fire has been used effectively to control invasive late season annual broadleaf and grass species, particularly yellow starthistle (*Centaurea solstitialis*), medusahead (*Taeniatherum caput-medusae*), barbed goatgrass (*Aegilops triunciallis*), and some brome grasses (*Bromus* spp.). A limited number of invasive biennial broadleaves [i.e., sweetclover (*Melitotus* spp.) and garlic mustard (*Alliaria petiolata*)], perennial grasses [i.e., bluegrasses (*Poa* spp.) and smooth brome (*Bromus inermis*)], and woody species [i.e., brooms (*Cytisus* spp.) and Chinese tallow (*Triadica sebifera*)] have also been successfully controlled with fire. The most success comes when fire is integrated with other control strategies (i.e., herbicides, mechanical) within an integrated pest management framework.

Most scientific studies have focused on the responses of specific invasive plants and largely disregard how other species or the plant community responds as a whole. This lack of information is a major problem for land managers because the ultimate reason for controlling invasives in the first place is to reduce the dominance of the invasive species and increase the dominance of the desired native species. Other objectives may include increasing the status and/or health of endangered plants, wildlife and insect populations, and hydrologic function. If these results are not achieved, then using fire to control target invasive plant infestations may not be worth the effort.

Land managers considering using fire to control invasive plants should be careful to examine the characteristics of the target invasive species. The survival rate of plants depends on the degree to which reproductive tissues are protected from a fire's lethally high temperatures. Plants with reproductive tissues located below ground (i.e., seeds or tubers) have higher survival rates and tend to recover more quickly than plants with vegetative tissues located above ground (i.e., many shrubs and trees) (Table 1).

Table 1. Effects of fire on different plant life forms (modified from Pyke et al. in prep).

Life Form (Raunkiaer type)	Regenerative tissue	Exposure of regenerative tissue to damage from fire
Annual plants	Seeds that reside on or under the soil surface, or on dead plants	Depends on if seeds are located above-ground on the parent plant, or at or below the soil surface after they have dispersed from the parent plant.
Bulbs or corms	Living tissue well below the soil surface	Protected from fire due to soil insulation above them.
Rhizomatous plants	Living tissue just above or below the soil surface	Depends on the percentage of litter burned and the amount of smoldering combustion.
Shrubs	Living tissue just above the soil surface	Non-fire-adapted shrubs can be killed by fire due to their positioning directly in the flame zone of surface fires.
Trees	Living tissue well above the soil surface	Can be killed by crown fire that passes though the plant canopies, or by surface fire that girdles the trees.

3. Plant Invasions Can Affect Fuels, Fire Behavior, and Fire Regimes

One significant way that invasive plants can affect the areas they are invading is by changing fuel properties, which then affects fire behavior (Table 2). If the altered fuel properties remain or increase after burning, then the fire regimes may be altered. When altered fire regimes promote the spread of the invaders that cause the changes in the first place, then the system is considered to be in an invasive plant / fire regime cycle.

There are four phases that lead to the establishment of an invasive plant/fire regime cycle:
Phase 1 involves the initial spread of invasive plants into an area.

Phase 2 is characterized by establishment of self-perpetuating populations of the invasive plant.

Phase 3 occurs when the plant spreads beyond the area first infested, especially disturbed sites into less disturbed wildland sites, and begins to negatively impact surrounding native plant communities.

Phase 4 results in fuel properties being changed to the point that the natural fire regime shifts. If the new fire regime favors the spread of the invasive species and reduces the native species, an invasive plant/fire regime cycle becomes established (Fig. 3). The most well-known effects of plant invasions on fire regimes involve those that increase the frequency, intensity, or length of the fire season. Collectively, these changes increase what are commonly referred to as "fire hazards." For example, annuals grasses that have invaded shrublands can increase the frequency of fire and the length of the fire season in the western United States, and invaders that increase the woody fuel load can increase fire intensity in the southeastern United States. In addition, invading plants with high tissue flammability (i.e., Eucalyptus) can ignite easier and burn more intensely.

Plant invasions don't always increase fire hazards, and in some cases can actually reduce them. Invasions can make fuelbeds less flammable by increasing live fuel moisture, decreasing fuel continuity, or decreasing fuel loads (Table 2). Examples are harder to find because managers are generally less concerned about decreased fire hazards than they are about increased fire hazards. Potential examples include succulents (i.e., cactus and iceplant spp.) invading shrublands and increasing live fuel moisture, or trees that shade out surface vegetation and reduce surface fuel continuity.

Table 2. Primary effects of fuelbed changes on fire regimes. *

Fuelbed Change	Fire Regime Change
Increased amount (load)	Increased fire intensity and seasonal burn window; increased likelihood of crown fire
Decreased amount (load)	Decreased fire intensity and seasonal burn window; decreased likelihood of crown fire
Increased horizontal continuity	Increased fire frequency and extent
Decreased horizontal continuity	Decreased fire frequency and extent
Increased vertical continuity	Increased likelihood of crown fire
Decreased vertical continuity	Decreased likelihood of crown fire
Change in packing ratio	Change in fire frequency, intensity, and seasonality
Increased plant tissue flammability	Increased fire frequency, intensity, and seasonal burn window
Decreased plant tissue flammability	Decreased fire frequency, intensity, and seasonal burn window

* Modified from Brooks et al. (2004) Table 1

As fire regimes and other ecosystem properties become altered, restoration of pre-invasion conditions becomes increasingly more difficult and costly. As the invasive plant infestation spreads and alters the fire regime, the number of management actions and cost to restore native ecosystem functions increases, while the probability of success decreases. This is because restoration can ultimately require managing fuel conditions, fire regimes, native plant communities and other ecosystem properties, in addition to the invaders that caused the changes in the first place.

As with other ecological impacts caused by plant invasions, the most cost effective way to prevent the establishment of an invasive plant / fire regime cycle is to take preventative steps early on in the process.

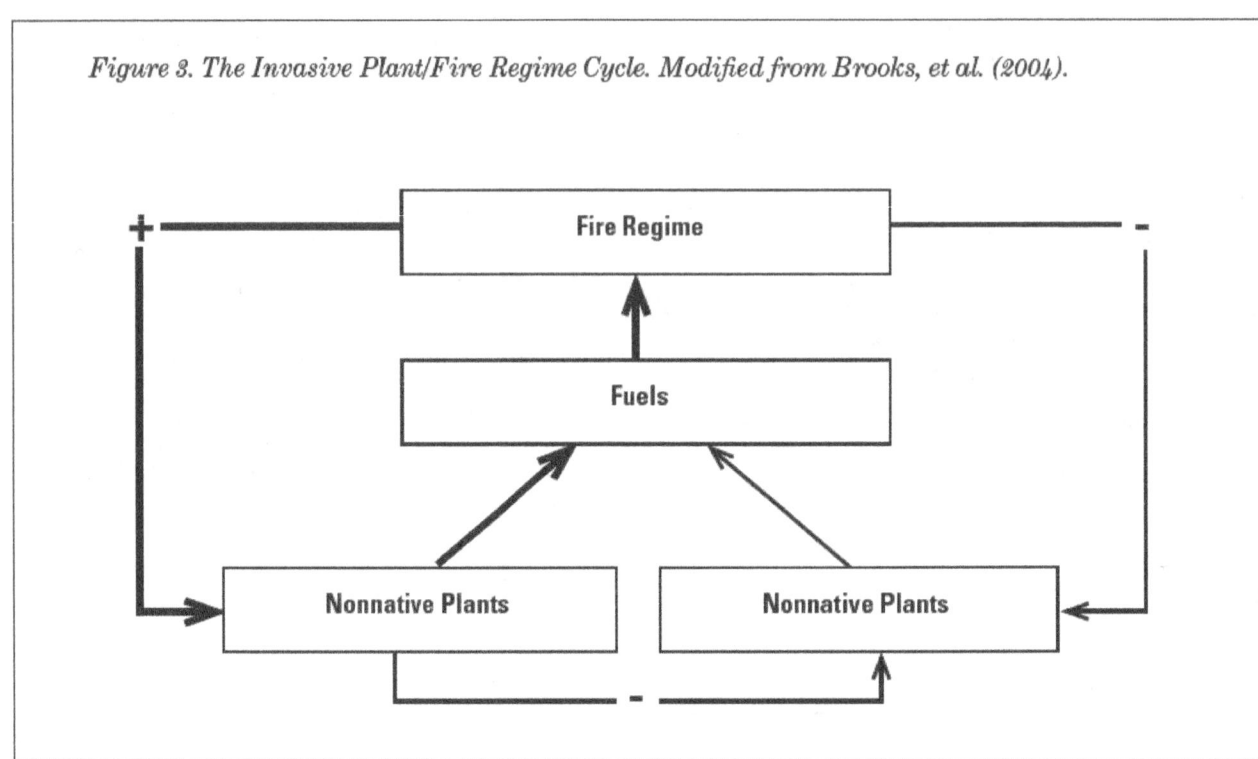

Figure 3. The Invasive Plant/Fire Regime Cycle. Modified from Brooks, et al. (2004).

Prescribed burn on Buffelgrass (Pennisetum ciliare) *on the Lower Rio Grande NWR. Photo by South Texas Fire District, USFWS.*

Section V
General Operational Guidelines for Fire Management

General guidelines have recently been published for reducing the spread and dominance of invasive plants in postfire landscapes (Asher et al. 2001, Goodwin et al. 2002, Keeley 2003). Collectively these publications present the following general recommendations: 1) in response to individual fires, procedures should be implemented to reduce inadvertent dispersal of weeds into or within the burned area; 2) areas where invasive plants of particular concern are likely to invade or increase in dominance should be targeted for control efforts; 3) additional revegetation treatments of other species may be effective at competing with the target invasives by reducing resource availability; and 4) National Environmental Policy Act (NEPA) analyses that are likely to be required prior to implementing postfire control treatments (i.e., herbicide use) should be completed and ready to use before the fire season. A Pesticide Use Plan (PUP) is also required before herbicides can be approved for use.

Although these existing guidelines are helpful, they are basically checklists of do's and don'ts, and there is always the chance that situations may arise where appropriate guidance is not found on one of the lists. For example, these guidelines generally focus on fire suppression and postfire emergency stabilization, rehabilitation, and restoration activities, and do not address issues associated with fuels management. They also do not explicitly integrate fire management with other land management programs during the years leading up to and following fires, nor do they provide specific guidance on prioritizing which actions may be most effective in a given situation.

The approach of this handbook is to explain the primary mechanisms associated with plant invasions (i.e., resource availability and propagule availability), and provide examples of how their effects can be mitigated to minimize invasion potential. With a basic working understanding of the invasion

Prescribed fire for standing-dead salt cedar. Photo by M. Weisenberger, USFWS.

process, a land manager can then better evaluate how best to integrate fire management actions (preparedness, suppression, wildland fire use, prescribed fire, hazardous fuels and post-wildfire recovery treatments,) into overall land management, especially when they encounter situations that are not described in existing guidelines. This knowledge will also help land managers prioritize the prevention steps that are most important for reducing invasion potential in their particular situation. Examples are provided below that focus on minimizing plant propagules and resource availability, using the conceptual model presented earlier in this document (Figs. 1 and 2). In later sections the conceptual model is applied to managing invasive plants in the context of specific fire management activities.

Minimizing Propagule Availability

Propagule availability can be reduced by ensuring that seeding treatments do not include species that may become management problems in the future (Table 3). Careful consideration of all the problems associated with introductions of both nonnative plants, and native species outside of their native ranges, is the easiest way to reduce invasive species. Regional lists of invasive plants can be consulted to help inform fire managers of plants to avoid.

A much greater challenge involves managing propagule availability due to accidental dispersal of invasive plants from outside of a management unit (Table 3). This includes both long-distance dispersal from outside of the management unit and short-distance dispersal from adjacent areas, some of which may lie within the management unit. Sources of long-distance dispersal include vehicles and other mechanized equipment, personal items (clothes, boots, camping equipment), livestock from distant locations, seed mixes or other vegetation stock, and erosion control materials from distant locations (i.e., soils, rock, hay mulch). These sources are connected primarily to human transportation, so control can be focused where they enter the management unit of interest (i.e., fire camps, erosion control project areas). Short-distance dispersal from adjacent areas is much more difficult to manage than long-distance dispersal, because sources and pathways include all

of the above plus mechanisms such as wind, water, wildlife, human foot traffic, and other localized human activities.

The challenge in managing invasions that arise from outside of a management unit is in detecting and eradicating the new invaders before they establish local populations. Necessary steps to detect and eradicate these new invaders include reducing dispersal rates, detecting newly established individuals, and eradicating them. Each of these steps is potentially very costly, so land managers need to evaluate how to get the most "bang for the buck."

Minimizing Resource Availability

One of the most obvious recommendations for reducing the likelihood an area will be invaded is to reduce resource inputs such as adding nitrogen or phosphorous to the soil (Table 3). Second only to soil moisture, these nutrients are often the primary limiting factors of plant growth. It may seem like a good idea to add these nutrients to give native vegetation some help as they recover from a fire event, but unfortunately invasive plants can often take advantage of large increases in nutrient availability more effectively than native plants. Increased invasive plant biomass fueled by nutrient additions creates additional water demands, and can lead to increased competition for soil moisture. For similar reasons, the use of nitrogen-fixing plants which can increase available soil nitrogen should be used with caution in revegetation treatments.

Resource availability can also be reduced by maximizing resource uptake (Table 3). This can be done by retaining existing vegetation as much as possible in fuels treatments. For example, if hazard fuels reduction can be achieved by only removing ladder fuels, while retaining surface and canopy fuels, then the potential for subsequent plant invasion should be lower than if surface fuels or surface and canopy fuels are removed as well. Resource uptake can also be accomplished by adding vegetation in postfire emergency rehabilitation projects. Carbon sources, such as organic mulches, can help reduce levels of available nitrogen.

Table 3. General recommendations for minimizing the potential for plant invasions following fire and fire management actions.

Plant Propagules

Prevent deliberate dispersal

Carefully evaluate plants considered for use in revegetation projects to ensure that they are unlikely to become management problems in the future.

Minimize accidental dispersal

Decontaminate equipment by washing after use and/or before using at a new geographic location.

Implement an early detection and rapid response plan during the first 3 years following fire to detect and eradicate new populations of invasive plants within the management unit.

Implement a control and monitoring plan during the first 3 years following fire to keep existing invasive plant populations from spreading within the management unit.

Plant Resources

Minimize resource input

Avoid using nitrogen or phosphorous soil amendments

Avoid revegetating with nitrogen-fixing plants (i.e., legumes)

Maximize resource uptake

Reduce loss of vegetation biomass

Promote the re-establishment of desirable vegetation, either through direct seeding, planting or implementation of appropriate land-use regimes (i.e., temporary closures to grazing)

Use carbon sources (i.e., organic mulches) to reduce available soil nitrogen.

Section VI
Specific Operational Guidelines for Major Fire Management Activities

Fuels Management

Fuel management practices can also lead to the proliferation of invasive plants. Fuels management almost universally involves removal of plant biomass, which has the potential to increase nutrient availability and thus increase the likelihood an area will be invaded. Crews and equipment used for fuels treatments also have the potential to spread invasive plants. The window of opportunity for invasions largely depends on how long it takes for native vegetation to recover compared to the time invasive plants become established and spread.

Once established, invasive plants can create new and unexpected fire hazards that may be even more difficult to manage. Even fuel treatment specifically targeted to remove an invasive plant [e.g., salt cedar (*Tamarix* spp), or giant reed (*Arundo donax*)] can be followed by invasion of another species that, in turn, could bring additional problems. Monitoring for new invasive plants following the fuels treatments may be necessary.

Recommendations for lessening the possibility that a fuels management treatment may increase the spread of invasive plants apply to the degree that project goals can still be achieved (i.e., establishment of a managed fuel zone). Evaluating what is required to achieve fuels management goals requires analyses beyond the scope of this handbook (i.e., fire behavior modeling).

Plant propagules

If the locations of invasive plants are known prior to planning a fuel treatment then those locations can be avoided when possible. The effect of fuels treatments on nutrient availability may be tempered by whether or not potentially invasive plants are nearby. For example, invasive plants may spread after a fuel treatment where past disturbances left a large number of invasives, but not where there were few invasives prior to the treatment.

Unfortunately, invasive plants are often associated with roads and trails which are commonly used as anchor points for fuels treatments.

Fuels Management Treatments
Best management practices for minimizing the potential for plant invasions

Reducing Propagule Availability
Ensure that vehicles, equipment, and personnel do not spread invasive plants into the project site.

Avoid incorporating pre-existing invasive plant populations into managed fuel zones.

Implement a monitoring and control plan for invasive plants after the fuels treatments are applied.

Identify populations of invasive plants within the project area and focus control efforts in those areas.

Reducing Resource Availability
Minimize vegetation removal while still accomplishing fuels management objectives.
- Target only the fuel layers that typically carry fire (i.e., the understory and ladder fuels in a forest).
- Selectively thin to reduce fuel continuity rather than clear-cut.
- Construct fuel breaks no wider than necessary to accomplish fuel reduction objectives.

Consider revegetating with less flammable vegetation following removal of flammable vegetation.

Cover exposed soil with an organic mulch (i.e., hydromulch or chipped fuels).

Incorporate pre-existing fuel breaks, either man-made or natural (i.e., areas of bare rock), into managed fuel zones.

Care is taken to limit burning near roads where no invasive plants are present. Photo by M. Weisenberger, USFWS.

Plant resources

Fuels treatments can involve the complete or partial removal of plant biomass. The greater the percentage of existing vegetation that is removed, the greater the potential for spread of invasive plants. For example, cover of invasive plants often increases with the proportion of overstory vegetation that is removed. Also, treatments that involve both fuels thinning and burning can lead to higher invasive plant cover than treatments that include one or the other individually.

In some cases fuels management may include adding plant cover of low flammability, commonly called greenstripping. This technique involves the strategic planting of low flammability plants to prevent or reduce the rate of fire spread. It has been used effectively by the Bureau of Land Management in the Intermountain West. An added benefit of greenstripping is its potential to reduce nutrient availability for invasive plants such as cheatgrass *(Bromus tectorum)*. However, the benefits of adding potentially aggressive greenstripping plants (which are typically nonnative) to reduce fire spread and compete with other undesirable species such as cheatgrass *(Bromus tectorum)* must always be weighed against the potential negative effects of the species (i.e., competition with natives or other ecosystem impacts). More information on greenstripping can be found at http://fresc.usgs.gov/research.

Fire Suppression

Over time, invasive plants can pose even greater management challenges than the fires themselves. The recommendations below are designed to reduce the likelihood for fire suppression activities to create opportunities for invasive plants to become established. These recommendations should only be considered when there is no immediate threat to human life and/or property.

Plant propagules

Fire suppression activities are more likely to influence propagule availability than resource availability. Fire-fighting crews and their equipment can move invasive plants as they travel. Firefighters set up small camps and their equipment largely consists of personal belongings (i.e., boots, clothes, sleeping bag, tent), Personal Protective Equipment (PPE)(i.e., nomex gloves, helmet, goggles, fire pack, fire shelter), back-pack sprayers, and hand tools (i.e., shovels, pulaskies, axes, fire rakes, hoes). This equipment can help spread invasive plants unless they are cleaned prior to use at other locations. At the very least, fire-fighters should clean tools, boots, and tents prior to arriving and leaving a fire site.

Heavy equipment such as bulldozers probably have the greatest potential for spreading invasives because they often accumulate significant amounts of soil and vegetation debris in their undercarriages. When heavy equipment is used, it should either be washed prior to transport or washed before it is allowed to operate in new wildland areas.

Aircraft are often used to transport and disperse water, foam, or other fire retardant. These aircraft may be helicopters with buckets, or fixed-wing aircraft known as tankers or scoopers. There is some concern that helicopters or scoopers could carry invasive plants in the water they use. Aquatic or riparian plants are most likely to be transported in this manner, and because they are most likely to be deposited into upland sites where most fires occur, they would likely not become established. A significant exception may be the potential for establishment in springs and creeks that are often common in upland areas. In general, the likelihood of moving invasive plants long distances by this method is probably low because water is typically obtained from local sources near fires.

Plant resources
Fire suppression activities rarely lead to increased resource availability, although there are a few notable exceptions. For example, the use of phosphate-based fire retardants may lead to increased growth of invasive plants where phosphate is a limiting nutrient. The construction of fuelbreaks and some firelines, both by handcrews and by heavy equipment, could lead to increased nutrient availability due to reduced rates of consumption from plants that are removed to clear the line.

Backing fires could have similar results for the same reasons. More temporary control lines such as wet lines or foam lines may be less likely to encourage plant invasions because the existing vegetation is left in place.

Emergency Stabilization, Rehabilitation, and Restoration

Plant propagules
Seed mixes and application equipment are potential sources for invasive plants. Seed mixes should be inspected to ensure they are "weed free." This may require testing sub-samples to determine their species composition before they are applied. Application equipment also needs to be cleaned before and after use, especially if equipment was previously used in areas with known invasive plant infestations.

Plant resources
Plants are mostly seeded after fires to stabilize soils, but in some cases they are seeded to compete with and suppress invasive plants. For example, nonnative wheatgrasses (*Agropyron* spp.) have often been planted to suppress the growth of cheatgrass in the Intermountain West.

Jeff Olson at the Prescribed Fire Training Center. Photo by Greg Zoppetti, USFWS.

Fire Suppression
Best management practices for minimizing the potential for plant invasions

Reducing Propagule Availability
Ensure that vehicles, equipment, and personnel do not spread invasive plants into burned areas.

- Coordinate with local personnel who know the locations of invasive plants or who can quickly survey sites for their presence.

- Include warnings to avoid known areas infested with invasive plants during briefings at the beginning of each shift.

- Avoid establishing staging areas (i.e., fire camps, helibases) in areas dominated by invasive plants.

- If populations of invasive plants occur within or near staging areas, flag their perimeters so that vehicle and foot traffic can avoid them.

- Inspect vehicles and equipment and wash them if they have invasive plants or materials that may contain invasive plants (i.e., mud) on them. Inspections should be done when vehicles first arrive at the fire, and periodically during the fire as they return from working in the field.

Avoid the use of water from impoundments infested with invasive plants.

Identify populations of invasive plants within the burned area and focus postfire control efforts in those areas.

For pre-planned wildland fire, environmental assessments should at least document the locations of major populations of invasive plants within the proposed burn unit and evaluate the potential for the burn prescription to increase their dominance and spread. If the potential is high, either remove those areas from the burn unit or develop a postfire mitigation plan.

Implement a postfire monitoring and control plan for invasive plants. Focus on populations of invasive plants known to exist before the fire and on areas of significant fire management activity during the fire (i.e., fire camps, dozer lines).

Reducing Resource Availability
Minimize vegetation removal in the construction of control lines.

- Use wet lines and foam lines as much as possible.

- Use narrow handlines rather than broad dozer lines or blacklines.

Minimize the use of nitrogen and phosphate-based retardants, except where their use eliminates the need for vegetation removal.

Tie control lines into pre-existing fuel breaks and managed fuel zones.

During mop up, scatter organic matter back over exposed soil where control lines were established.

Emergency Stabilization, Rehabilitation, and Restoration
Best management practices for minimizing the potential for plant invasions

Reducing Propagule Availability
Ensure that vehicles, equipment, and personnel do not spread invasive plants into the project site.

Revegetate with native species, or nonnatives that are not likely to become invasive.

Test seed mixes or other types of revegetation materials to ensure that they do not contain invasive plants as contaminants.

Implement a monitoring and re-treatment plan for invasive plants after the initial treatments are applied.

Reducing Resource Availability
Vegetate with fast-growing but non-invasive plants to increase the uptake of resources that would otherwise be utilized by invasive plants.

Cover exposed soil with an organic mulch (i.e., hydromulch or chipped fuels).

Focus efforts on reducing resource availability in areas with sources of invasive plants.

Postfire Land-Use Regimes

Plant propagules

Any land-use activity increases the chance for accidental introduction of invasive plant, so reducing these activities can lessen the potential for plant invasions. Invasive plants can be moved by many ways, including people, stock animals, pets, vehicles, equipment, and livestock feed just to name a few. Thus, any person or anything traveling into a recently burned area should be considered a potential vector. It is much more cost effective to prevent plant invasions than to manage them after invasive plant populations are firmly established.

Plant resources

There are often significant demands to quickly re-establish prevailing land-use activities following fires. If these activities affect resource availability, they may increase the likelihood an area will be infested by invasive plants. For example, livestock grazing is a common land-use on public lands, and one of its main effects is the removal of plant biomass. Biomass removal generally reduces levels of competition and increases the availability of soil nutrients, thus increasing the potential for invasive plants to move into an area.

If it is possible to target grazing on invasive plants, then it may help counteract the effects of increased soil nutrients. However, the ability to control what livestock eat makes focusing on undesirable vegetation very difficult. In addition, repeated grazing in focused areas over longer periods of time can lead to other problems such as soil erosion and loss of native species diversity, and even short periods of deferred grazing may allow nonnatives to rise to dominance.

Postfire Land-Use Regimes
Best management practices for minimizing the potential for plant invasions

Reducing Propagule Availability
Ensure that vehicles, equipment, and personnel do not spread invasive plants into burned areas.

Consider temporary closure of public access to burned areas to of invasive plants.

Consider using livestock grazing to target invasive plants for short-term control.

Reducing Resource Availability
Minimize land uses that may reduce vigor of resprouting of native plants (i.e., livestock grazing).

Treating invasive plants with fire. Photo by M. Weisenberger, USFWS

Section VII
Effectiveness Monitoring

Monitoring management actions should focus on responses of immediate interest, but should also consider abiotic factors. In most cases, monitoring is associated with the management action of interest (i.e., the influence of fuels management on fuel characteristics). Monitored responses will sometimes extend to secondary effects (i.e., the influence of fuels management on fuel characteristics, and ultimately on fire behavior and fire regimes). At a minimum, monitoring needs to determine whether objectives of the management action have been achieved.

Commonly used agency monitoring publications, described in Table 4, outline vegetation monitoring methodology, although none specifically address invasive plants. Monitoring plans should include the following elements: objectives, stratification, controls, random sampling, data quality, and statistical analysis. All of these topics, except for controls, are discussed at length in the publications listed in Table 4; only two monitoring publications (USDI National Park Service 2003, Lutes et al. 2006) cover all six monitoring elements.

Table 4. Agency publications on monitoring.

Monitoring Publication	Covers Fire Monitoring	Associated Software
Fish and Wildlife Service *Fuel and Fire Effects Monitoring Guide (USDI Fish and Wildlife Service 1999)*	Yes	No
Bureau of Land Management *Sampling Vegetation Attributes (Interagency Technical Reference 1999)*	No	No
National Park Service *Fire Monitoring Handbook (USDI National Park Service 2003)*	Yes	Yes
Forest Service *FireMon: Fire Effects Monitoring and Inventory Protocol (Lutes et al. 2006)*	Yes	Yes
Agricultural Research Service *Monitoring Manual for Grassland, Shrubland, and Savanna Ecosystems (Herrick et al. 2005a,b)*	No	Yes

Section VIII
Bibliography

Asher, J.E., S. Dewey, C. Johnson and J. Olivarez. 2001. Reducing the spread of invasive exotic plants following fire in western forests, deserts, and grasslands (abstract). *In:* Galley KEM and Wilson TP (Eds) Proceedings of the Invasive Species Workshop: the Role of Fire in the Control and Spread of Invasive Species. Fire Conference 2000: the First National Congress on Fire Ecology, Prevention, and Management, pp 102-103. Tall Timbers Research Station, Tallahassee, FL.

Brooks, M.L. C.M. D'Antonio, D.M. Richardson, J. Grace, J. J. Keeley, DiTomaso, R. Hobbs, M. Pellant, and D. Pyke. 2004. Effects of invasive alien plants on fire regimes. BioScience 54:677-688.

Brooks, M.L. 2007. Effects of land management practices on plant invasions in wildland areas. Pages 147-162 *in:* W. Nentwig (ed.) Biological Invasions. Ecological Studies, Vol. 193, Springer, Heidelberg, Germany.

Champion, P.D., and J.S. Clayton. 2001. A weed risk assessment model for aquatic weeds in New Zealand. Pages 194-202 *in* R.H. Groves, F.D. Panetta, and J.G. Virtue (eds.), Weed risk assessment. CSIRO, Collingwood, Victoria, Australia.

D'Antonio, C.M. and P.M. Vitousek. 1992. Biological invasions by exotic grasses, the grass/fire cycle, and global change. Annual Review of Ecology and Systematics. 23:63-87.

D'Antonio, C.M. 2000. Fire, plant invasions and global changes. *In:* H. Mooney and R. Hobbs (Eds). Invasive species in a changing world, pp. 65-94. Island Press, Covela.

DiTomaso, J.M., M.L. Brooks, E. B. Allen, R. Minnich, P. M. Rice, and G. B. Kyser. 2006. Control of invasive weeds with prescribed burning. Weed Technology 20:535-548.

DiTomaso, J. M. and D. W. Johnson (Eds.). 2006. The Use of Fire as a Tool for Controlling Invasive Plants. Cal-IPC Publication 2006-01. California Invasive Plant Council: Berkeley, CA. 56 pp.

Fox, A. M., D.R. Gordon, J.A. Dusky, L. Tyson, and R.K. Stocker. 2001. IFAS assessment of non-native plants in Florida's natural areas. SS-AGR-79. Agronomy Department, Florida Cooperative Extension Service, Institute of Food and Agricultural Sciences, University of Florida. Available online at http://agronomy.ifas.ufl.edu/docs/IFASAssessment2001.pdf

Galley, K. E. and Wilson. 2001. Proceedings of the Invasive Species Workshop: The Role of Fire in the Control and Spread of Invasive Species. Fire Conference 2000: The first National Congress on Fire Ecology, Prevention and Management, San Diego, CA, Misc. Pub No. 11.

Godwin, K., R. Sheley, and J. Clark. 2002. Integrated Noxious Weed Management After Wildfires. Montana State University Extension Service. 26 pp. Available online at www.montana.edu/wwwpb/pubs/eb160.html.

Heffernan, K.E., P.P. Coulling, J.F. Townsend, and C.J. Hutto. 2001. Ranking invasive exotic plant species in Virginia. Natural Heritage Technical Report 01-13. Virginia Department of Conservation and Recreation, Division of Natural Heritage: Richmond, Virginia. 27 pages. Avalable online at http://www.dcr.state.va.us/dnh/rankinv.pdf

Herrick, J.E., J.W. Van Zee, K.M. Havstad, L.M. Burkett, and W.G. Whitford. 2005a. Monitoring Manual for Grassland, Shrubland, and Savanna Ecosystems. Volume 1: quick start. USDA-ARS Jornada Experimental Range. Las Cruces, NM. 36 p.

Herrick, J.E., J.W. Van Zee, K.M. Havstad, L.M. Burkett, and W.G. Whitford. 2005b. Monitoring Manual for Grassland, Shrubland, and Savanna Ecosystems. Volume 2: design, supplementary methods and interpretation. USDA-ARS Jornada Experimental Range. Las Cruces, NM. 200 p.

Hiebert, R.D., and J. Stubbendieck. 1993. Handbook for Ranking Exotic Plants for Management and Control. U. S. Department of the Interior, Natural Resources Report NPS/NRMWRO/NRR-93/08. National Park Service, Natural Resources Publication Office, Denver, CO.

Interagency Technical Reference. 1999. Sampling Vegetation Attributes. BLM Technical Reference 1734-4. National Business Center, Denver, CO. 158 p

Keeley, J.E. 2003. Fire and invasive plants in California ecosystems. Fire Management Today 63:18-19

Klinger, R.E. Underwood, P. Moore. 2006. The role of environmental gradients in non-native plant invasion into burnt areas of Yosemite National Park, California. Diversity and Distributions 12: 139-156.

22

Lutes, D. C., R.E. Keane, J.F. Caratti, C.H. Key, N.C. Benson, S. Sutherland, and L.J. Gangi., 2006. FIREMON: Fire Effects Monitoring and Inventory System. Gen. Tech. Rep. RMRS-GTR-164-CD. For Collins, CO: U.S. Department of Agriculture, Forest Service, Rocky Mountain Research Station. 1 CD. 400 p.

Morse, L.E., J.R. Randall, N. Benton, R. Hiebert, and S. Lu. 2004. An invasive species assessment protocol: Evaluating non-native plants for their impact on biodiversity. Version 1, NatureServe, Arlington Virginia. Available online at http://www.natureserve.org/getData/plantData.jsp.

Orr, R.L., S.D. Cohen, and R.L. Griffin. 1993. Generic nonindigenous pest risk assessment process. U.S. Department of Agriculture, Washington, D.C.

Pyke, D., M. Brooks, C.M. D'Antonio. In prep. Fire as a restoration tool: a life form decision framework for predicting the control or enhancement of plants using fire. Restoration Ecology.

Thorp, J.R., and R. Lynch. 2000. The determination of weeds of national significance. National Weeds Strategy Executive Committee, Launceston, Australia. Avalable online at http://www.weeds.org.au/docs/WONS/

USDI Fish and Wildlife Service. 1999. Fuel and Fire Effects Monitoring Guide. http://www.fws.gov/fire/downloads/monitor.pdf. Accessed 9/22/06.

USDI National Park Service. 2003. Fire Monitoring Handbook. Fire Management Program Center, National Interagency Fire Center. Boise, ID. 274 p.

Virtue, J.G., R. H. Groves, and F.D. Panetta. 2001. Towards a system to determine the national significance of weeds in Australia. Pages 124-152 in R.H. Grove, F.D. Panetta, and J.G. Virtue, eds., Weed risk assessment. CSIRO, Collingwood, Victoria, Australia.

Warner, P.J., C.C. Bossard, M.L. Brooks, J.M. DiTomaso, J.A. Hall, A. Howald, D.W. Johnson, J.M. Randall, C.L. Roye, M.M. Ryan, and A.E. Stanton. 2003. Criteria for Categorizing Invasive Non-Native Plants that Threaten Wildlands. California Exotic Pest Plant Council and Southwest Vegetation Management Association. 24 pp. (http://ucce.ucdavis.edu/files/filelibrary/5319/6657.doc).

Weiss, J., and D. McLaren. 1999. Invasive Assessment of Victoria's State Prohibited, Priority and Regional Priority Weeds. Keith Turnbull Research Institute, Agriculture Victoria, Frankston, Victoria, Australia. 16 pp.

Wirth, Troy A., and Pyke, David A. 2007, Monitoring post-fire vegetation rehabilitation projects-A common approach for non-forested ecosystems: U.S. Geological Survey Scientific Investigations Report 2006-5048, 36 pp.

Zouhar, K., J. Kapler Smith, S. Sutherland, and M. L. Brooks. (eds.) 2008. Wildland fire in ecosystems: fire and nonnative invasive plants. Gen.Tech. Rep. RMRS-GTR-42-volume 6. Ogden, UT: U.S. Department of Agriculture, Forest Service, Rocky Mountain Research Station. 355 pp.

Using drip torches to apply fire to buffelgrass on the Lower Rio Grande Valley National Wildlife Refuge. Photo by South Texas Fire District, USFWS.

Appendix A.
Laws, Policies And Planning Documents Guiding the Management of Invasive Plants and Fire

Federal Mandates

The following is a chronological list of federal laws, executive orders and management plans pertaining to invasive plant control with fire management activities on federal lands. Federal Acts may be found on-line at: http://www.gpoaccess.gov/uscode/search.html; or Public Laws (since 1994) at: http://www.gpoaccess.gov/plaws/search.html.

National Wildlife Refuge System Administration Act, as amended
This act establishes the Fish and Wildlife Refuge System. This act requires the agency to administer lands to provide for the conservation of fish, wildlife, plants and their habitats and to ensure that biological integrity and diversity are maintained.

National Environmental Policy Act (1970)
This act requires government agencies to consider the environmental effects of their actions through the preparation of appropriate NEPA documents (i.e., EAS, EA or EIS). Effects of nonnative species, if harmful to the environment, would be included in NEPA analysis. In emergency situations, NEPA procedures that would normally be required may be negotiated with the Council of Environmental Quality.

Endangered Species Act (1973)
This Act protects federally listed Threatened and Endangered species. When nonnative invasive species threaten a Threatened or Endangered species, this Act could be used to justify treatment of the infestation.

Federal Land Policy and Management Act (1976)
This act establishes public land policy and guidelines for its administration and to provide for the management, protection, development, and enhancement of public lands.

Lacey Act (1981)
Under this Act it is unlawful to import, export, transport, buy or sell fish, wildlife and plants taken or possessed in violation of federal, state or tribal laws.

Using fire as a beneficial tool to treat invasive plants. Photo by M. Weisenberger, USFWS

Hawaii Tropical Forest Recovery Act (1992)

This Act establishes the Hawaii Tropical Forest Recovery Task Force to draft a plan for rejuvenating Hawaii's tropical forests.

Executive Order 13112 (1999)

This Order defines invasive species as an alien species whose introduction does or is likely to cause economic or environmental harm or harm to human health. It directs all federal agencies to address invasive species concerns and refrain from actions that are likely to increase invasive species problems. This Order also established the National Invasive Species Council and the development of a National Invasive Species Management Plan to better coordinate efforts among federal agencies.

Plant Protection Act (2000)

This Act replaced many previous invasive plant species acts including the Federal Noxious Weed Act, the Plant Quarantine Act, the Federal Plant Pest Act and other related statutes and primarily applies to USDA, but authorizes APHIS to take both emergency and extraordinary actions to address incursions of noxious weeds which can be regulated on federal lands.

Noxious Weed Control and Eradication Act (2004)

This Act is an amendment to the Plant Protection Act above and provides for the provision of funds through grants and agreements to weed management entities for the control and eradication of noxious weeds.

National Invasive Species Council Management Plan (2008)

The National Invasive Species Council was established by Executive Order 13112. One of its directives under the EO is to prepare a management plan for invasive species that will provide guidance for all federal agencies over a four year period.

Department of Interior Policy

The Departmental Manual (DM) has several policies addressing invasive species management issues. The following is numerically ordered list of DM policies that relate directly or indirectly to fire and invasive species management activities. DM policies may be found on-line at: http://elips.doi.gov/app_dm/index.cfm?fuseaction=home

516 DM 2 - Initiating the NEPA Process (2005)

This purpose of this Chapter is to provide instructions for implementing CEQ regulations that pertain to initiating the NEPA process. Appendix 2.12. states that the introduction of invasive species is an extraordinary circumstance to a Categorical Exclusion according to the Federal Noxious Weed Control Act and Executive Order 13112.

- Appendix 1 provides a list of management actions that are DOI Categorical Exclusions pursuant to 516 DM 2.3(A). Included in these actions

are: 1.6 - non-destructive inventory, research and monitoring activities, 1.12 - Hazardous fuels reduction activities using prescribed fire not to exceed 4,500 acres, and 1.13 - Post-fire rehabilitation activities not to exceed 4,200 acres.

- Appendix 2 lists Extraordinary Circumstances for some actions covered under Categorical Exclusions. Relevant actions include: 2.3 - Have highly controversial environmental effects, 2.4 - Involve unknown environmental risks, and 2.12 - Contribute to the introduction or spread of non-native invasive species.

516 DM 8 - Managing the NEPA Process - U.S. Fish and Wildlife Service (2004)

This Chapter provides supplementary requirements for implementing provisions of 516 DM 1 through 6 within the Department's U.S. Fish and Wildlife Service. Section 8.5 lists important Categorical Exclusions for FWS activities. Relevant Categorical Exclusions that may cover some fire and invasives management actions include:

- 8.5.B(1): Research, inventory, and information collection activities.
- 8.5.B(3): The construction... structures and improvements for the restoration of wetland, riparian, instream, or native habitats, which result in no or only minor changes in the use of the affected local area.
- 8.5B(4): The use of prescribed burning for habitat improvement purposes.
- 8.5B(5): Fire management activities, including prevention and restoration measures.
- 8.5B(6): The reintroduction or supplementation (e.g., stocking) of native, formerly native, or established species into suitable habitat within their historic or established range.

517 DM 1 Integrated Pest Management Policy (2007)

This policy updates the Integrated Pest Management (IPM) policy to make it consistent with current laws, contemporary science, and other authorities. The revised policy addresses the IPM process and pest management tools, including pesticides and biological control agents.

522 DM Implementation of Adaptive Management Policy (2008)

This Chapter provides guidance to help Agencies incorporate adaptive management strategies into their land and resource management decisions. Section 1.5 (B) requires offices to conduct appropriate monitoring to determine resource status and evaluate progress toward achieving objectives.

606 DM 2 Soil and Moisture Conservation Policy (1971)

This policy affirms that the purpose of the soil conservation program is to restore and maintain soil properties for optimal conditions. Both burning and weed control are listed as an appropriate soil and moisture conservation activities for site improvement (Section 2.2.B.1).

609 DM 1 Weed Control Program Policy (1995)

This policy defines undesirable plants/weeds as noxious when they interfere with man's activities or welfare. It is DOI policy to control undesirable plants on lands under its jurisdiction. Further, programs within DOI for the control of undesirable plants will incorporate integrated pest management practices. DOI Bureaus will coordinate their integrated pest management activities with other federal and non-federal agencies where possible. At the Bureau level, each Bureau is responsible for planning, funding, implementing, and overseeing integrated pest management programs. This policy establishes the DOI weed control committee with representatives from each bureau and is charged with overall interdisciplinary program development.

620 DM 2 Burned Area Rehabilitation Policy (2004)

This chapter provides the Departmental Policy for the Emergency Stabilization and Rehabilitation on Bureau lands and Indian Trust Lands following wildland fires. Specifically, Section 3.8E states that exotic species introductions as a part of seeding in burned areas are restricted with exceptions from the Secretary of the Interior. Section 3.2.W. states that Executive Order 13112 is an authority for conducting BAER activities. Other references to the prevention of invasive species are found throughout this Chapter.

Fish and Wildlife Service Policy

There are many citations throughout the Fish and Wildlife Service Manual (FW), Administrative Manual (AM) and Refuge Manual (RM) that describe FWS policy as it relates to invasive species. The following is a list of FWS and NWRS policies directly or indirectly related to invasive species and fire management activities. FWS policies may be found on-line at: http://www.fws.gov/policy/manuals/.

Environment 30 AM 12 Pest Management Policy and Responsibilities

This policy affirms that the FWS will use integrated pest management in its planning of pest management actions. Section 12.5 (B) lists burning as a type of cultural control that can be used to reduce pest populations.

052 FW 4 Planning and Management

This policy states that the ecosystem approach concept to fish and wildlife management will be implemented. Section 1.8.B.2.a.vii. states that goals should include exotic species concepts when developing plans.

Fire can be an effective tool to restore habitat on a landscape scale. Photo by M. Weisenberger, USFWS.

095 FW 3 Emergency Operations

This policy involves fire management activities. Section 3.9.C.1.a. describes fire damage restoration to include the use of herbicides, and other site preparation activities to reduce weed competition prior to seeding burned areas for restoration. Section 3.9.B.2.E states that the FWS will minimize the establishment of nonnative species in BAER activities to prevent unacceptable degradation to burned areas, Section 3.D.1.C. states that fuels management projects will minimize the establishment of invasive species.

601 FW 1 National Wildlife Refuge System Mission and Goals and Refuge Purposes

This policy reiterates that the overarching goal of the NWRS is to conserve a diversity of fish, wildlife, and plants and their habitats by focusing on native species.

601 FW 3 Biological Integrity, Diversity and Environmental Health

This policy involves maintaining and restoring the biological integrity, diversity and environmental health of NWRs. Section 3.10.B3 states that the FWS strives to minimize the spread of invasive species; Section 3.11.B. states that the FWS should use physical structures and chemical applications to manage for biological diversity and eliminate invasive species; Section 3.14.F. states that the FWS supports the reintroduction of extirpated native species to control invasive species if needed; Section 3.16.A. states invasive species should not be introduced, populations should be detected and controlled through integrated pest management strategies including mechanical, chemical, biological, and cultural control methods.

602 FW 3 Exhibit 2 Comprehensive Conservation Planning

This exhibit describes the statutes that should be considered in the CCP process and identifies the Noxious Weed Act as a mandate.

603 FW 1 Appropriate Refuge Uses

This policy states that invasive species control is an accepted refuge management activity that is included in appropriate refuge uses (Section 1.2.B).

603 FW 2 Compatibility

This policy states that refuge management activity such as invasive species control does not require a compatibility determination (Section 2.10.A).

620 FW 1 Habitat Management Plans

This policy describes guiding principles for the development of habitat management plans on refuges. Section 1.4.E defines the term invasive species for habitat management plans; Section 1.7G describes guiding principles which should include invasive species management. Section 1.7.G. also states that an integrated pest management plan will be used to describe activities related to the control of invasive species

640 FW 1 Partners for Fish and Wildlife Program

This chapter describes the implementation of the Partners for Fish and Wildlife Program. Section 1.13.I on Service fire management policy recognizes that prescribed fire is an important and acceptable tool to remove exotic species and gives guidelines for using Partners funding for prescribed burning.

7 RM 8 Exotic Species Introduction and Management

This policy affirms that the NWRS exists for the protection and management of plants and animals native to the United States. It outlines the special circumstances under which the continued existence of nonnative plants or animals may be permitted. In particular, it discusses the requirements for releasing biocontrols onto a refuge.

7 RM 14 Pest Control

Although this policy deals largely with the use of pesticides on refuges, it does affirm that one of the objectives of pest management activities on refuges is to control exotic species and allow normal populations of native species to exist.

The National Strategy for Management of Invasive Species
National Wildlife Refuge System (2003)

This document was developed by a Fulfilling the Promise Team with the support of the regional refuge chiefs. It outlines a comprehensive strategy for dealing with the critical problem of invasive species on National Wildlife Refuges. The plan was developed in the context of Executive Order 13112 and the National Invasive Species Council management plan. A copy of this strategy may be found on-line at: http://www.fws.gov/invasives/pdfs/ NationalStrategyFinalRevised05-04.pdf